Oxford Firs
Thesaurus

OXFORD
UNIVERSITY PRESS

Great Clarendon Street, Oxford OX2 6DP

Oxford University Press is a department of the University of Oxford.
It furthers the University's objective of excellence in research, scholarship,
and education by publishing worldwide in

Oxford New York

Auckland Bangkok Buenos Aires Cape Town Chennai
Dar es Salaam Delhi Hong Kong Istanbul Karachi Kolkata
Kuala Lumpur Madrid Melbourne Mexico City Mumbai Nairobi
São Paulo Shanghai Taipei Tokyo Toronto

Oxford is a registered trade mark of Oxford University Press
in the UK and in certain other countries

British Library Cataloguing in Publication Data available

Hardback ISBN 0 19 910727 0
Paperback ISBN 0 19 910728 9

3 5 7 9 10 8 6 4

Typeset in Bembo Schoolbook
by Melissa Orrom Swan
Printed in Italy by G. Canale & C. S.p.A.

Oxford First
Thesaurus

Compiled by Andrew Delahunty
Illustrated by Steve Cox

OXFORD

UNIVERSITY PRESS

Preface for teachers and parents

The **Oxford First Thesaurus** introduces primary school children to the idea of a thesaurus and helps them develop the skills they need in using one. It is a tool that can be used to help build children's vocabulary and to add variety and liveliness to their writing. All the words have been carefully chosen and are the words young children will use most frequently in their writing. Special attention has been given to such overused words as **bad**, **big**, **do**, **get**, **go**, **good**, **nice**, and **say**.

This thesaurus is arranged alphabetically. There are three main types of entry. There are entries that give synonyms. These are words that are close in meaning to the headword. Each synonym is supported by a definition or example sentence to help children choose the most appropriate word. At the headword **eat** for example, the different meanings of **bite**, **chew**, **gobble**, **munch**, **nibble**, and **taste** are explained. Sometimes the headword has two or more different meanings. So under the headword **hard**, words that mean 'not soft' and also words meaning 'not easy' are included.

There are also entries that give related words. For example, under the headword **water**, the related words **flow**, **pour**, **splash**, **drip**, and **trickle** are listed. Under the headword **farm**, animals and other things you find on a farm are listed. Then there are topic entries that give lists of different kinds of things. For example, under the headword **bird**, you will find **chicken**, **magpie**, **parrot**, **pelican**, and **swan**.

Remember a thesaurus is not the same as a dictionary. A thesaurus does not necessarily give you explanations or definitions of what words mean. If you want to know what a word means, you may need to look it up in a dictionary such as the *Oxford First Dictionary*.

Using a thesaurus can be fun; we hope children will enjoy using this thesaurus to find a voice of their own in their writing. The colour illustrations support the entries and draw very young readers into the book. The text has greatly benefited from extensive trialling in primary schools. The author, illustrator, and publishers are most grateful to all those teachers whose comments and suggestions have helped make this book as useful as possible.

How to use the thesaurus

What is a thesaurus for?

A thesaurus is a kind of dictionary that puts together words that have a similar meaning. It helps you to choose just the right word for what you want to say or write. It also helps you to try using new and different words rather than using the same words all the time.

Headwords

The **headword** is in colour at the top of each page. It is the starting point for finding other useful words. The headwords are arranged alphabetically. The **alphabet** appears at the side of the page to help with alphabetical order.

Synonyms

The **synonyms** are in thick blue text. They have a similar meaning to the headword. If you look at the headword **soft**, you can see that the words **fluffy**, **squashy**, and **floppy** all have meanings similar to 'soft'.

Definitions

Definitions tell you what words mean. They are often given for the headwords. Definitions are also given for many of the synonyms to help you choose the right word for what you want to say or write. The definition for **fluffy** tells you that something that is fluffy has soft hair, fur, or feathers.

Example sentences

Example sentences show how you use the word in a sentence. The example sentence for the word **fluffy** is *A fluffy yellow chick hopped out.*

Antonyms

Some words have opposite meanings, called **antonyms**. You can sometimes find these at the bottom of the page. If you look at the bottom of the page that has the headword **soft**, you can see that its opposite or antonym is **hard**.

Related words

Related words are useful words for talking or writing about a subject given for some headwords. Under the headword **space**, you can find words such as **spaceship**, **astronaut**, **moon**, and **planet**.

Topic entries

If you look up the headword **book** you will find different books listed such as **atlas**, **diary**, **dictionary**, and **thesaurus**.

Index

If you want to find a word quickly in the thesaurus try looking in the index at the back. This lists all the headwords in the thesaurus in alphabetical order, with their page numbers.

Making your writing more interesting

Imagine you are writing about what you did at the weekend. You might start like this:

> I had a nice day on Saturday. The weather was nice so we went to a nature park. The lady who showed us round was very nice. We saw lots of nice animals, including some deer. I had a nice chocolate ice cream.

Can you see how the word **nice** is used over and over again? It would be more interesting if you sometimes used another word instead. If you look up **nice** in the thesaurus you will find other words you can choose which have a similar meaning. So you could write this instead:

> I had an enjoyable day on Saturday. The weather was fine so we went to a nature park. The lady who showed us round was very friendly. We saw lots of nice animals, including some deer. I had a delicious chocolate ice cream.

These are the main features in the thesaurus:

alphabet

headword —→ **hot**

When something is **hot**, it burns if you touch it.
Careful, that pan is hot!

definition —→ If something is **warm**, it is quite hot.
Jo loves her cosy warm bed.

If you feel **hot**, you are too warm.
Josh felt hot and thirsty.

example
sentence

These words mean very hot.

baking blazing boiling

burning scorching sweltering

synonym

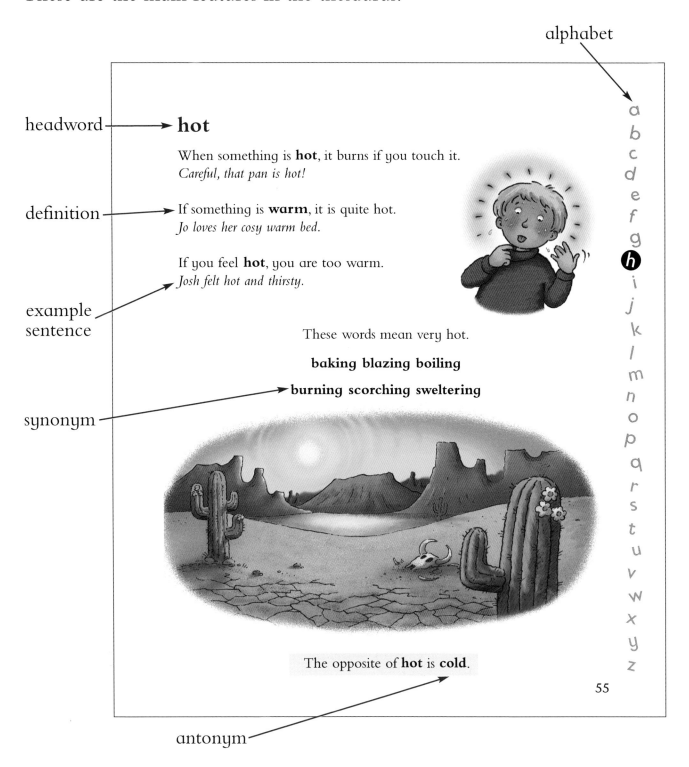

The opposite of **hot** is **cold**.

antonym

a b c d e f g **h** i j k l m n o p q r s t u v w x y z

55

7

angry

If someone is **angry**, they are not pleased at all with what someone has done or said.
The giant looked so angry Jack decided to run away.

You can also say that they are **annoyed** or **cross**.
Jack's mother is cross with him for being late.

If someone is **furious** or **in a rage**, they are very angry.
The giant is furious that Jack has stolen his treasure.

If someone **loses their temper**, they become angry all of a sudden.
Someone who is **bad-tempered** or **grumpy** is often in a bad mood.
Why are you so grumpy today?

bad

Bad is a very common word and it has a lot of different meanings. You can often use another word instead.

What a bad child!
You could say **naughty** instead.

The king was a bad man.
You could say **wicked** instead.

She is bad at spelling.
You could say **poor** instead.

There's a bad smell coming from the dustbin.
You could say **nasty** or **revolting** or **horrible** instead.

I feel bad about forgetting his birthday.
You could say **awful** or **dreadful** or **terrible** instead.

The opposite of **bad** is **good**.

beautiful

You say someone or something is **beautiful** if you enjoy looking at them or listening to them.
What a beautiful rainbow!

Here are some other words you can use.

lovely
The princess sang a lovely song.

pretty
She wore a pretty dress.

handsome
A handsome knight listened to her singing.

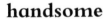

sweet
'What a sweet voice!' he said.

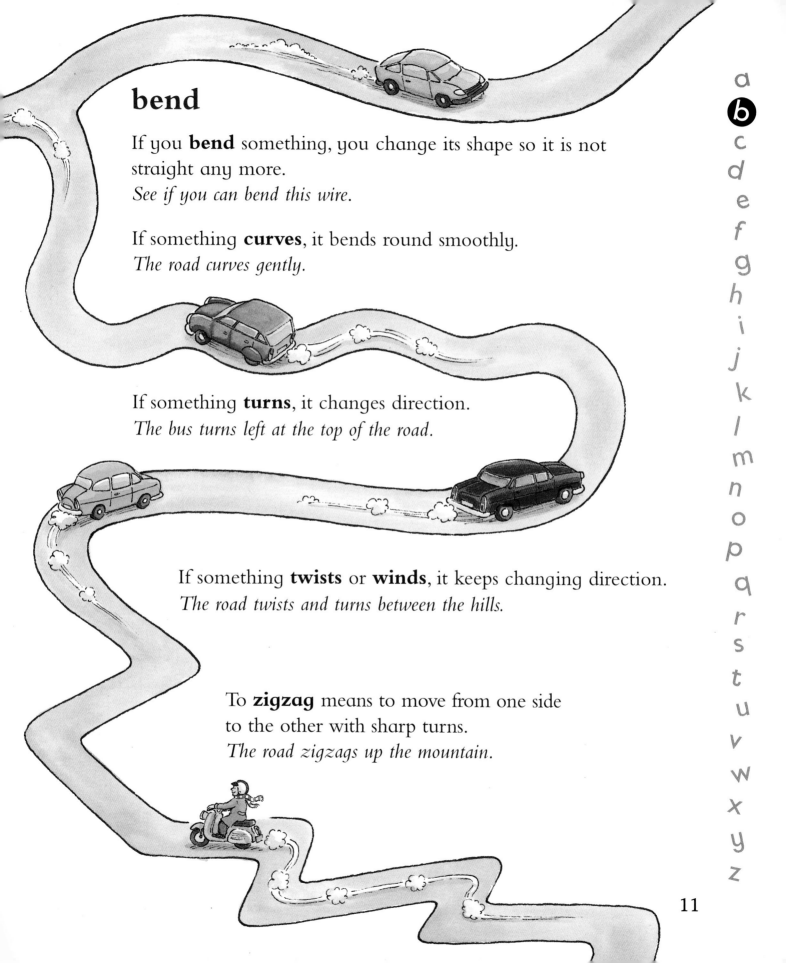

bend

If you **bend** something, you change its shape so it is not straight any more.
See if you can bend this wire.

If something **curves**, it bends round smoothly.
The road curves gently.

If something **turns**, it changes direction.
The bus turns left at the top of the road.

If something **twists** or **winds**, it keeps changing direction.
The road twists and turns between the hills.

To **zigzag** means to move from one side to the other with sharp turns.
The road zigzags up the mountain.

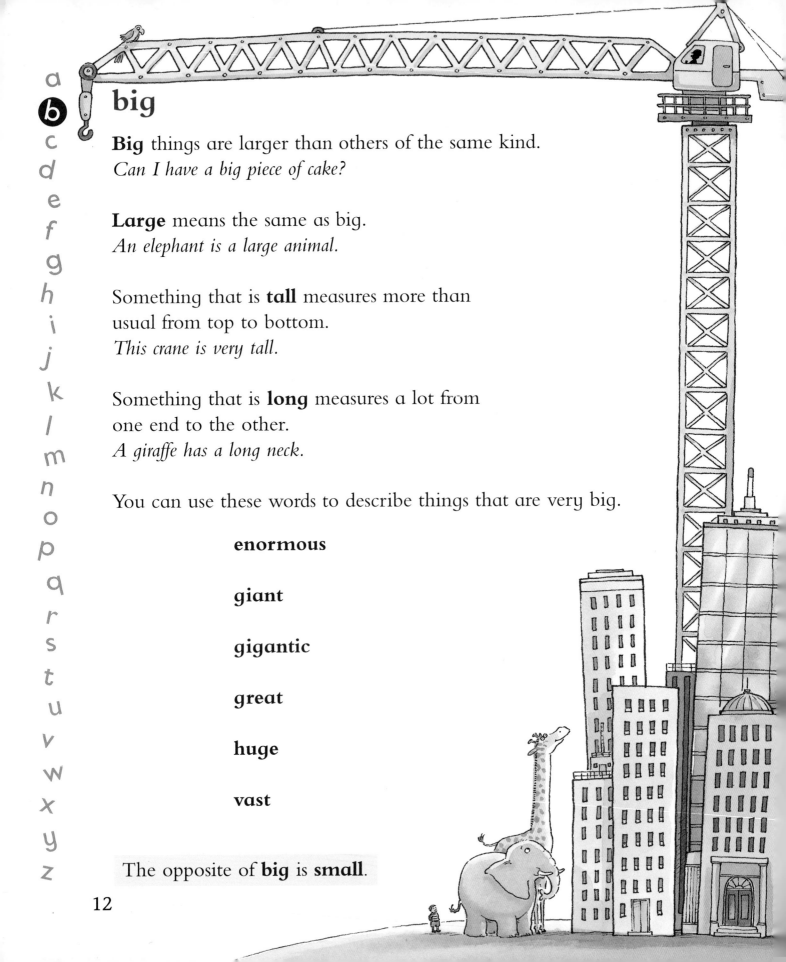

big

Big things are larger than others of the same kind.
Can I have a big piece of cake?

Large means the same as big.
An elephant is a large animal.

Something that is **tall** measures more than
usual from top to bottom.
This crane is very tall.

Something that is **long** measures a lot from
one end to the other.
A giraffe has a long neck.

You can use these words to describe things that are very big.

enormous

giant

gigantic

great

huge

vast

The opposite of **big** is **small**.

a b c d e f g h i j k l m n o p q r s t u v w x y z

12

bird

These are all different kinds of bird.

budgerigar

chicken

eagle

magpie

owl

parrot

pelican

penguin

pigeon

robin

swan

woodpecker

13

book

Here are words for different kinds of book.

An **album** is a book in which you can keep photographs or stamps.

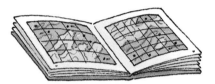

An **atlas** is a book of maps.

A **diary** is a book in which you can write down what happens each day.

A **dictionary** is a book where you can find out what a word means and how to spell it.

An **encyclopedia** is a book or set of books containing information about lots of different things.

A **thesaurus** is a book that gives you sets of words that all have a similar meaning.

brave

If you are **brave**, you show that you are not afraid.
The brave knight rode up to the dragon's cave.

These words also mean brave.

bold

courageous

daring

fearless

The opposite of **brave** is **cowardly**.

break

If something **breaks**, it goes into pieces or stops working.
You can use these words to talk about different things breaking.

If something **cracks**, it has a line in it where it is
broken but does not break in to pieces.
The plate cracked down the middle.

If it **snaps**, it breaks suddenly with a
sharp cracking noise.
He hung on to the branch until it snapped.

If it **bursts**, it breaks open suddenly.
The football burst so we had to stop playing.

If it **splits**, it tears or cracks open.
Your trousers have split at the back!

If it **pops**, it breaks open with a small bang.
The balloon popped.

If it **smashes**, it breaks into lots of pieces
with a loud noise.
She picked up a brick and smashed the window with it.

If it **shatters**, it breaks suddenly into tiny pieces.
The mirror fell to the floor and shattered.

change

When things **change**, they become different.
Caterpillars change into butterflies.

When something **turns** into something else, it changes.
The frog turned into a handsome prince.

You can also say that one thing **becomes** something else.
As the sun goes down, the blue sky becomes pink.

If you **switch** something, you change it and put
something else in its place.
Do you mind if I switch channels?

If you **swap** something, you give it to someone in
return for something else.
Can we swap seats so I can look out of the window?

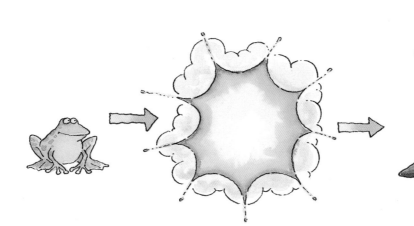

clean

When you **clean** something, you get all the dirt or stains off.
You can use these words to talk about different ways of cleaning.

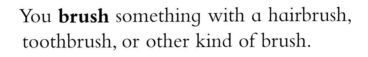

You **brush** something with a hairbrush, toothbrush, or other kind of brush.

You **dust** something with a duster.

You **rinse** something in clean water.

You **scrub** something with a hard brush.

You **sweep** something with a broom.

You **wash** something with water and soap.

You **wipe** something with a cloth.

18

clever

Someone who is **clever** learns and understands things easily.
These words also mean clever.

bright

intelligent

brainy

Brilliant means very clever indeed.

Someone who is **wise** knows and understands many things.
Someone who is **cunning** is clever at deceiving people.

a
b
c
d
e
f
g
h
i
j
k
l
m
n
o
p
q
r
s
t
u
v
w
x
y
z

clothes

These are all different kinds of clothes.

blouse

cardigan

coat

dress

jacket

jumper

knickers

pyjamas

shirt

shorts

skirt

sweatshirt

trousers

underpants

20

cold

If you are **cold**, you feel that you want to put on warm clothes, or stand near something warm.
The weather got very cold and it began to snow.

If something is **cool**, it feels quite cold.
I'd like a cool drink.

These words also mean cold.

chilly *It was a chilly day.*

freezing *Can we go back in? I'm freezing!*

frozen *Lucy's fingers were frozen.*

icy *An icy wind was blowing.*

The opposite of **cold** is **hot**.

colour

These are all different kinds of colour.

black

blue

brown

green

grey

orange

pink

purple

red

violet

white

yellow

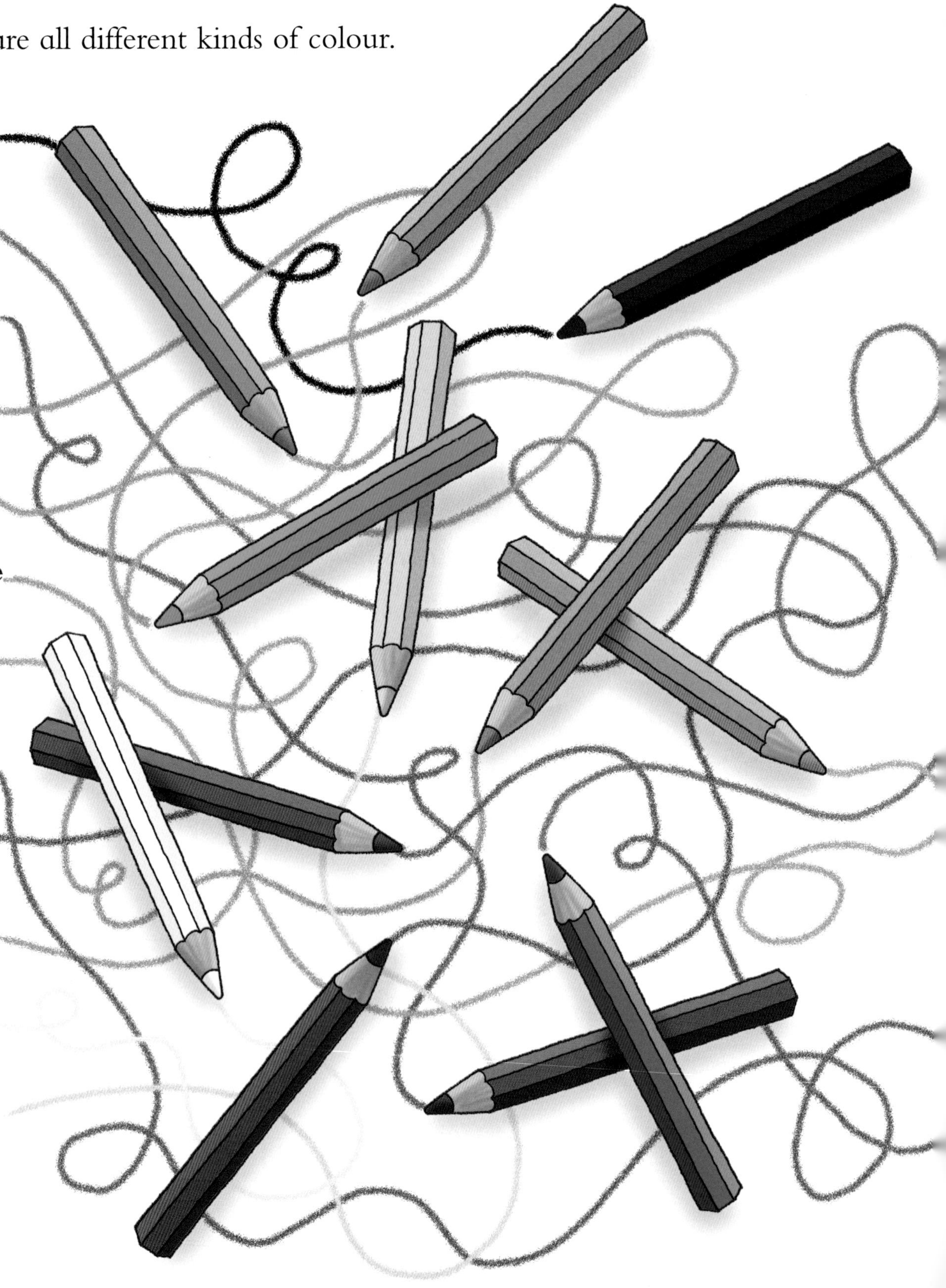

computer

Here are some words you can use if you are talking or writing about your computer.

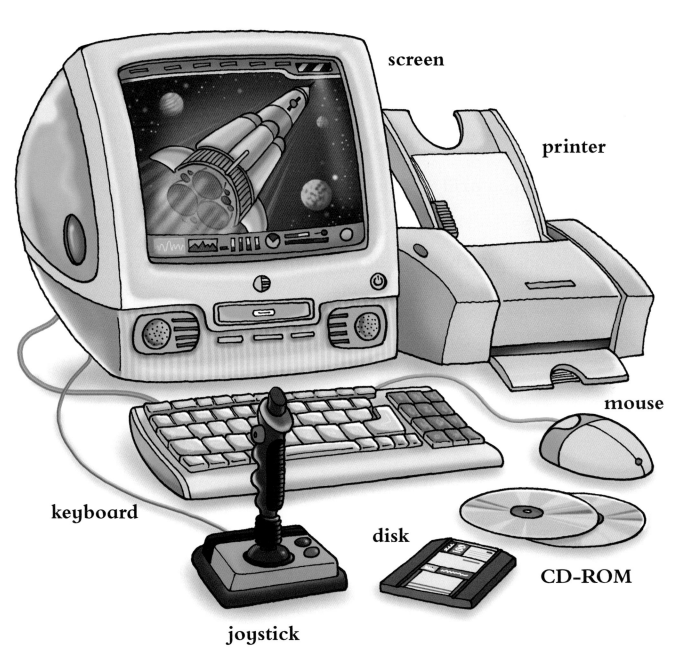

screen

printer

mouse

keyboard

joystick

disk

CD-ROM

cook

If you **cook** something, you get it ready to eat by heating it. You can use these words to describe different ways of cooking.

When you **bake** something, you cook it in an oven. You can bake bread and cakes.

When you **boil** something, you cook it in boiling water.

When you **fry** something, you cook it in hot fat in a pan.

When you **grill** something, you cook it over or under a flame or heated surface.

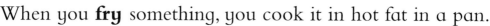

When you **poach** fish or an egg without its shell, you cook it in or over boiling water.

When you **roast** something, you cook it in an oven or over a fire. You can roast meat.

When you **scramble** eggs, you cook them by mixing them up and heating them in a pan.

When you **stew** something, you cook it slowly in liquid.

When you **toast** something, you cook it by heating it under a grill or in front of a fire.

cut

If you **cut** something, you use scissors or a knife.
Here are some words you can use for cutting different things.

You **carve** meat.

You **chop** wood with an axe.

You **mow** the lawn.

You **saw** wood.

You **shave** with a razor.

You **slice** bread.

You can **trim** your hair.

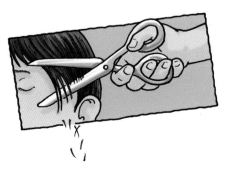

damage

If a person or thing **damages** something, they do something to it so that it is not as good as it was before.
The storm damaged our roof.

If something **breaks**, it goes into pieces or stops working.
Don't drop your glasses as you might break them.

If you **scratch** something, you damage it by moving something sharp over it.
Be careful you don't scratch the table.

If you **burn** something, you damage it with fire and heat.
Dad's burnt the toast again.

If you **destroy** something, you damage it so badly it cannot be used again.
Many houses were destroyed in the fire.

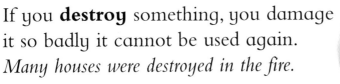

Ruin and **wreck** mean the same as destroy.

dirty

Something that is **dirty** is covered with mud, food, or other marks.
Josh came in from the garden with a dirty face.

Dusty means covered with dust.
These shelves are dusty.

Muddy means covered with mud.
Take your muddy boots off.

If something is **smudged**, it is marked with streaks of dirt.
The mirror is smudged.

These words mean very dirty.

filthy

grubby

mucky

The opposite of **dirty** is **clean**.

do

Do is a very common word and it has a lot of different meanings. You can often use another word instead.

Samir said he would do some animal masks for everyone.
You could say **make** instead.

Don't forget to do all your homework.
You could say **finish** instead.

Will five big sheets of paper do?
You could say **be enough** instead.

We are going to do the animal kingdom at school today.
You could say **learn about** instead.

easy

If something is **easy**, you can do it or understand it without any trouble.
This story is easy to read.

Simple means the same as easy.
The instructions are simple.

If something is **plain**, it is easy to see or understand.
The meaning is plain.

If something is **clear**, it is easy to see, hear, or understand.
Speak in a clear voice.

If something is **obvious**, it is very easy to see or understand.
The answer to the riddle is obvious.

The opposite of **easy** is **hard** or **difficult**.

eat

When you **eat**, you take food into your mouth and swallow it.
You can use these words to talk about different ways of eating.

If you **bite** something, you use your teeth to cut into it.

When you **chew** food, you break it up between your teeth.

To **gobble** means to eat something quickly and greedily.

To **munch** means to chew something noisily.

To **nibble** means to take tiny bites.

To **taste** means to try a little bit of food to see what it is like.

These words are to do with animals.

To **gnaw** means to keep biting something which is hard.
The dog gnawed the bone.

To **graze** means to eat grass.
Cows graze in the field.

To **peck** means to eat something with a beak.
Hens peck at the corn.

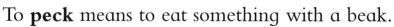

end

The **end** is the last part of something.
We read the story right to the end.

Here are some other words that mean the last part of something.

ending *The film has a sad ending.*

finish *The race had a very exciting finish.*

The **back** of something is the part furthest from the front.
She was right at the back of the queue.

The **end** of something that has a long shape is one of the parts furthest away from the middle.
The knight looked at the end of the dragon's tail.

The **tip** is the pointed end of something.
The dragon's tail had a pointed tip.

When something **ends** or **finishes**, it comes to the end.
We went to bed before the film ended.

When something **stops**, it finishes happening.
Has the rain stopped yet?

When you **break up**, you reach the end of a school term.
We break up for the summer next week.

face

Your **face** is the front part of your head where
your eyes, nose, and mouth are.
Your **expression** is the look on your face.

You can use these words to describe different
expressions on a person's face.

When you **frown**, you wrinkle your forehead
because you are angry or worried.

When you **glare**, you look angrily at someone.

When you **grin**, you smile showing your teeth.

When you **scowl**, you look bad-tempered.

When you **smile**, your face shows that you are feeling happy.

fall

When something **falls**, it comes down suddenly.
Leaves fall from the trees in autumn.

If something **drops**, it falls. If you **drop** something, you let it fall.
Don't drop the cake!

If something **sinks**, it goes downwards, usually under water.
The ship is sinking.

If you **trip**, you fall over something.
Kieran tripped over a rock.

To **topple** means to fall over.
That pile of acorns is about to topple.

To **tumble** means to fall over or fall down.
Jill tumbled down the hill.

If something **collapses**, it falls to pieces.
The bridge collapsed under the weight of so many elephants.

farm

Here are some words you can use if you are talking or writing about a farm.

Parts of a farm

barn

cowshed

farmhouse

farmyard

pigsty

stable

Machines you use on a farm

combine harvester

milking machine

plough

tractor

Animals you find on a farm

bull

calf

chicken

cow

goat

hen

horse

lamb

pig

sheep

Plants that farmers grow

barley

oats

wheat

a b c d e f g h i j k l m n o p q r s t u v w x y z

find

When you **find** something that has been lost, you get it back.
Ben tried to find his pencil sharpener.

When you **discover** something, you find it.
The explorers discovered a golden statue in the jungle.

If you **spot** something, you notice it by looking hard for it.
See if you can spot the needle in the haystack.

If you **look** for something, you try to find it.
Jenny looked for her cat.

When you **search** or **hunt**, you look very carefully for something.
I've searched everywhere for my red shoes,
but I can't find them.

If you **seek** something, you
try to find it.
Let's play hide and seek.

fire

Fire is the heat and bright light that comes from things that are burning.

A **flame** is one of the hot, bright strips of light that rise up from a fire.

You also get **smoke**.

If something is **burning**, it is on fire.

A **fire** is something which keeps people warm. There are different kinds such as a **coal fire**, an **electric fire**, and a **gas fire**.

A **fireplace** is the part of a room where the fire is.

A **bonfire** is a fire which someone lights outdoors.

a b c d e f g h i j k l m n o p q r s t u v w x y z

flower

These are all different kinds of flower.

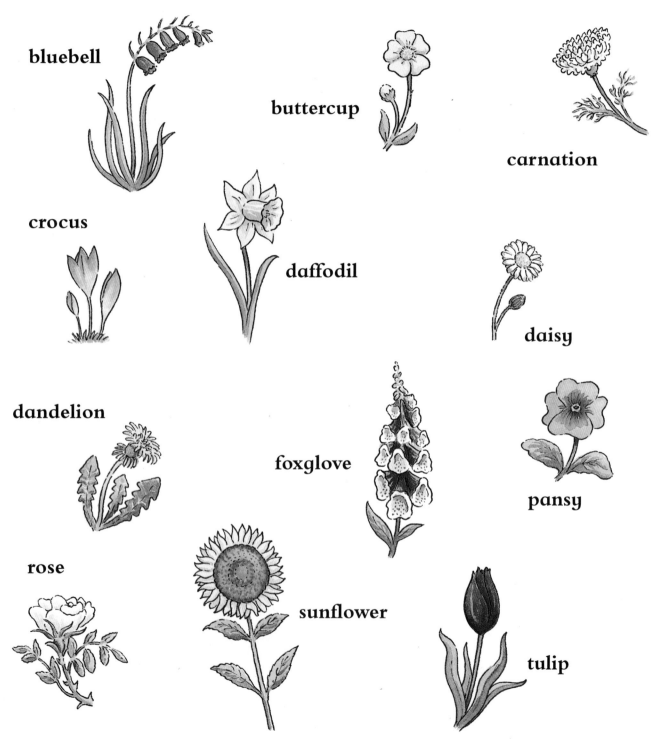

bluebell

buttercup

carnation

crocus

daffodil

daisy

dandelion

foxglove

pansy

rose

sunflower

tulip

fly

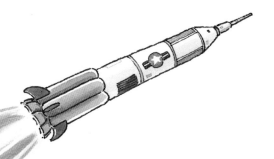

When things **fly**, they move through the air.

When a bird or butterfly **flaps** its wings, it moves them up and down or from side to side.

To **flutter** means to fly by flapping the wings quickly.
A butterfly fluttered in through the window.

When a bird **glides**, it flies smoothly without flapping its wings.

When a plane **glides**, it flies without an engine.

If something **hovers**, it stays in one place in the air.

To **soar** means to fly high in the air.
The rocket soared into the sky.

To **swoop** means to fly down suddenly.
The eagle swooped down.

If a bird or aeroplane **takes off**, it goes up into the air to begin flying.

frightened

Someone who is **frightened** or **scared** or **afraid** is worried that something bad might happen.
My brother Ian is frightened of spiders.

Someone who is **terrified** is very frightened.

If something **frightens** a person or animal, it makes them feel afraid.
The ghost train frightened both of us.

Scare means the same as frighten.

fruit

These are all different kinds of fruit.

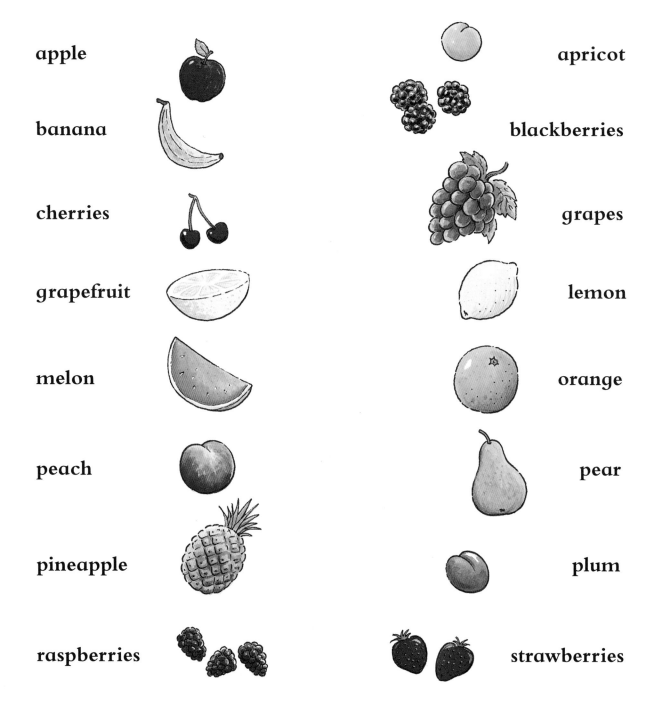

apple

banana

cherries

grapefruit

melon

peach

pineapple

raspberries

apricot

blackberries

grapes

lemon

orange

pear

plum

strawberries

full

If something is **full**, there is no more room in it.
The jar is full of sweets.

If a place is full of people, you can say that it is **crowded** or **packed**.
The hall is packed.

If something is very full, you can say that it is **crammed** or **bursting**.

The opposite of **full** is **empty**.

garden

Here are some words you can use if you are talking or writing about a garden.

Things you find or tools you use in the garden

flower bed
flowers
greenhouse
hedge
lawn
plants
pond
rockery
sandpit
shed
vegetables
weeds

fork
hoe
hose
lawn mower
rake
shears
spade
trowel
watering can

a b c d e f **g** h i j k l m n o p q r s t u v w x y z

get

Get is a very common word and it has a lot of different meanings. You can often use another word instead.

I hope I get a lot of birthday presents.
You could say **receive** instead.

Can we get some sweets on the way home?
You could say **buy** instead.

Get your sister from the garden.
You could say **fetch** instead.

Grandma, will you get me from school today?
You could say **collect** instead.

When did you get here?
You could say **arrive** instead.

Take a drink with you in case you get thirsty.
You could say **become** instead.

a
b
c
d
e
f
g
h
i
j
k
l
m
n
o
p
q
r
s
t
u
v
w
x
y
z

give

If you **give** something to someone, you let them have it.
Samir likes to give presents.

If you **offer** something, you hold it out
and ask someone if they would like it.
Tom went round the room, and offered everyone a biscuit.

If you **hand** something to someone,
you give it to them with your hand.
Will you hand me the phone?

If you **pass** something, you hand it
over to someone.
Please pass the butter.

If you **lend** something of yours to someone,
you let them have it for a short time.
Wendy is happy to lend me her watch.

A **present** is something you give to someone.

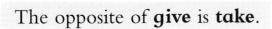

The opposite of **give** is **take**.

a b c d e f **g** h i j k l m n o p q r s t u v w x y z

45

go

Go is a very common word and it has a lot of different meanings. You can often use another word instead.

The children sing a song as they go down the lane.
You could say **walk** instead.

A racing car can go very fast.
You could say **travel** instead.

Is it time to go?
You could say **leave** instead.

Does this path go to the waterfall?
You could say **lead** instead.

Where did my bike go to?
You could say **disappear** instead.

My watch won't go.
You could say **work** instead.

Where do these coats go?
You could say **belong** instead.

Where does this piece go in the jigsaw?
You could say **fit** instead.

Put the milk in the fridge or it will go sour.
You could say **become** instead.

good

Good is a very common word and it has a lot of different meanings. You can often use another word instead.

This is a good book.
You could say **enjoyable** instead.

Be a good boy.
You could say **well-behaved** instead.

He was a good king.
You could say **kind** or **nice** instead.

There's a good smell coming from the oven.
You could say **nice** or **lovely** or **fine** instead.

This work is good.
You could say **well done** instead.

The opposite of **good** is **bad**.

a b c d e f **g** h i j k l m n o p q r s t u v w x y z

a b c d e f **g** h i j k l m n o p q r s t u v w x y z

group

A **group** is a number of people or things that belong together in some way.
A group of children were fishing.

A **set** is a group of things that belong together.
Bonnie has a new set of coloured pencils.

A **collection** is a group of things you have collected as a hobby.
Alex has a large collection of shells.

Here are some other words that mean a group of people or animals.

A **crowd** is a lot of people in one place.

A **club** is a group of people who meet together because they are interested in the same thing.

A **team** is a group of people who work together, or who play together on the same side.

A **band** is a group of people who play musical instruments together.

A **flock** is a group of sheep or birds.

A **herd** is a group of cows.

A **shoal** is a group of fish.

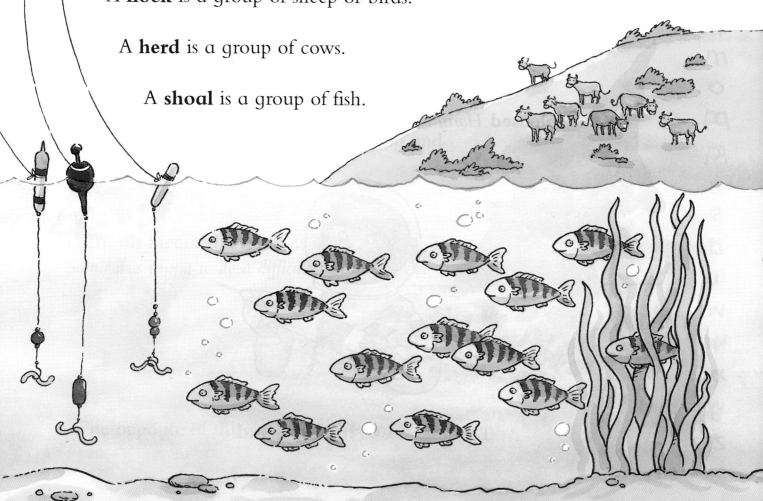

hole

A **hole** is a gap or opening in something.
These are some different kinds of holes.

A **cave** is a big hole under the
ground or inside a mountain.

A **burrow** is a hole
dug by a rabbit
or fox.

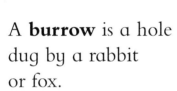

A **gap** is a space between things.
Quick, through that gap in the hedge!

A **tear** is a hole or split
in a piece of clothing.

A **tunnel** is a long hole
under the ground or
through a hill.

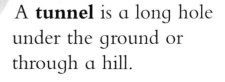

hot

When something is **hot**, it burns if you touch it.
Careful, that pan is hot!

If something is **warm**, it is quite hot.
Jo loves her cosy warm bed.

If you feel **hot**, you are too warm.
Josh felt hot and thirsty.

These words mean very hot.

baking blazing boiling

burning scorching sweltering

The opposite of **hot** is **cold**.

a
b
c
d
e
f
g
h
i
j
k
l
m
n
o
p
q
r
s
t
u
v
w
x
y
z

hurt

When you **hurt** part of your body, you feel pain.

If part of your body **aches**, it goes on hurting.

Something that is **sore** feels painful.
It must be awful to be a giraffe with a sore throat.

Bees and wasps can **sting** you.
The bear was stung on the nose by the bee.

A **bruise** is a dark mark on your skin where you have been hit or bumped yourself.

A **burn** is a sore place on your skin you get from something hot.

A **graze** is a sore place on your skin you get by rubbing against something.

56

insect

These are all different kinds of insect.

ant

bee

beetle

butterfly

cricket

dragonfly

fly

grasshopper

ladybird

wasp

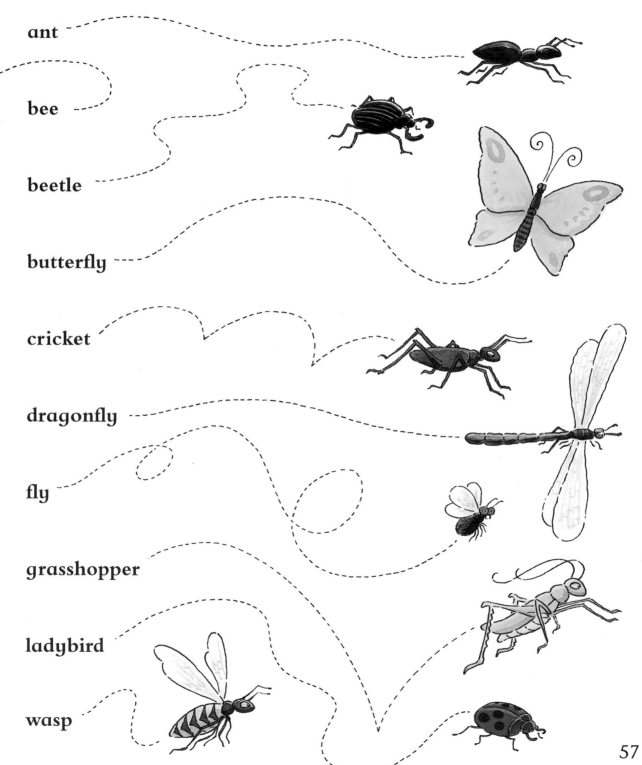

a b c d e f g h i j **k** l m n o p q r s t u v w x y z

know

When you **know** something, you have found it out and have it in your mind.
Billy is the only one who knows the answer.

When you **learn**, you get to know something you did not know before.
We've been learning about space.

When you **remember** something, you bring it back into your mind when you want to.
Do you remember the names of the nine planets?

When you **understand** something, you know what it means or how it works.
I don't understand the question about the moon.

laugh

When you **laugh**, you make sounds that show you are happy or think something is funny.

Cackle means to laugh loudly in a nasty way, like a wicked witch does.

Chuckle means to laugh quietly.

Giggle and **titter** mean to laugh in a silly way.

Roar with laughter means to laugh very loudly.

Snigger means to laugh in a quiet, sly way.

light

Here are some words you can use when talking or writing about what light does.

When something **shines**, it gives out light or looks very bright.
The moon shines on the water.

When it **flashes**, it shines suddenly and brightly, sometimes going on and off quickly.
The lights on the top of the buildings flash all night.

When it **flickers**, it shines in an unsteady way.
The candle flickered softly.

When it **glows**, it is bright and warm without flames.
The fire was glowing in the grate.

When it **gleams**, it shines with a soft light.
A cat's eyes gleam in the dark.

When it **glimmers**, it gleams faintly.
She saw the lights of the city glimmering in the distance.

When it **shimmers**, it shines with a faint quivering light.
The sea shimmered in the moonlight.

When it **glistens**, it shines like something wet or polished.
His eyes glistened with tears.

When it **dazzles**, it is so bright that it hurts your eyes.
The car headlights dazzled us.

When it **sparkles**, it shines with a lot of tiny flashes of bright light.
Diamonds sparkled in the candlelight.

When it **glitters**, it sparkles.
Her crown glittered with jewels.

When it **twinkles**, it sparkles.
Twinkle, twinkle, little star.

like

If you **like** someone or something, you think it is nice.
Do you like swimming?

If you **love** someone, you like them very much.
Eddie loves his pet cat Oscar.

If you **enjoy** something, you like doing it.
I really enjoy playing football.

If you **want** something, you would like to have it.
Anita wants some paints for her birthday.

If you **feel like** something, you want it.
I feel like an ice cream.

If you **prefer** something, you like it more than something else.
Which do you prefer, the red shirt or the blue shirt?

Your **favourite** is the one you like the most.
My favourite colour is blue, but Samir's is yellow.

look

When you **look**, you use your eyes.
Come and look at the parrot.

These are words for different ways of looking.

If you **gaze** at something, you look at it for a long time.
We lay on our backs, gazing at the stars.

If you **glance** at something, you look at it for a very short time.
The rabbit glanced at the kangaroo.

If you **peep** at something, you look at it quickly or secretly.
Jake peeped over the fence.

If you **stare** at something, you look at it for a time without moving your eyes.
It's rude to stare at people.

If you **watch** something, you look at it for a while.
The kangaroo watched Billy for ages.

loud

Something that is **loud** makes a lot of
sound and is easy to hear.
The music is too loud.

A **noise** is a loud sound.
What is that noise?

A lot of loud sound is **noisy**.
The room was full of noisy children.

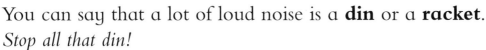

You can say that a lot of loud noise is a **din** or a **racket**.
Stop all that din!

Here are some other words for loud noises.

A **bang** is a sudden loud noise.

A **crash** is a very loud noise you hear
when something falls or breaks.

A **roar** is the loud sound that a lion makes.

The opposite of **loud** is **quiet**.

a b c d e f g h i j k **l** m n o p q r s t u v w x y z

make

To **make** means to get something new
by putting other things together.
It took Billy all day to make the robot.

If you **build** something, you make it by
putting parts together.
*This summer we are going to
build a tree house.*

If people **form** a shape, they sit
or stand in that shape.
Now let's form a circle.

Make has a lot of other different meanings.
You can often use another word instead.

Uncle Jim wants to make a little speech.
You could say **give** instead.

See if you can make the N into an M.
You could say **turn** or **change** instead.

Four and seven makes eleven.
You could say **add up to** or **equal** instead.

meal

A **meal** is the food eaten at different times of the day.
These are words for meals you can have.

A **snack** is a small meal.

You eat **breakfast** in the morning.

You eat **lunch** in the middle of the day.

You eat **dinner** as the main meal of the day.

You eat **tea** in the afternoon or early evening.

You eat **suppe**r as a meal or snack in the evening.

A **picnic** is a meal you eat in the open air away from home.

A **feast** is a special meal for a lot of people.

mean

If something you do is **mean** it is not kind to someone else.
That was a mean trick!

Unkind means the same thing.
Someone who is **nasty** is not at all kind.
Someone who is **spiteful** says or does horrid things to upset people.
Someone who is **cruel** enjoys hurting people or animals.
The king was a wicked and cruel ruler.

If someone tells you what a word **means**, they tell
you how to use it.
'What does gigantic mean?' 'It means very big.'

Someone who is **mean** does not like spending
money or sharing things.
Uncle Ebenezer was rich but very mean.

Someone who is **selfish** thinks only about themselves
and does not share things with other people.
Eating all the ice cream was a selfish thing to do.

The opposite of this last meaning of **mean** is **generous**.

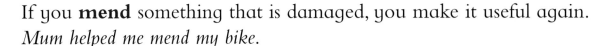

mend

If you **mend** something that is damaged, you make it useful again.
Mum helped me mend my bike.

If you **repair** something, you mend it.
Those men are repairing the roof.

If you **fix** something that is broken, you mend it.
Can you fix the radio?

If you **patch** something, you put a piece of material on it to mend it.
Mum patched my jeans.

If you **sew**, you use a needle and cotton.
Dad sewed the button back on his shirt.

mix

When you **mix** things, you stir or shake them until they become one thing.
You can make green by mixing blue and yellow.

When you **stir** something, you mix it by moving it round and round with a spoon.
The witch stirred her brew.

If things are **jumbled up** or **muddled up**, they are mixed up so that they are all in the wrong order.
All her clothes were jumbled up on the floor.

If you **shuffle** cards, you mix them up before you hand them out.

A **mixture** is made of different things mixed together.
Now pour the cake mixture into a tin.

nice

Nice is a very common word and it has a lot of different meanings.
You can often use another word instead.

The family next door are very nice.
You could say **friendly** instead.

It was nice of you to bring me a present.
You could say **kind** or **good** or **thoughtful** instead.

Did you have a nice time?
You could say **enjoyable** or **pleasant** instead.

It's a nice day today.
You could say **fine** or **lovely** or **sunny** instead.

You look very nice in that hat.
You could say **pretty** or **handsome** instead.

This cake is nice.
You could say **delicious** or **tasty** instead.

pet

A pet is a tame animal that you keep at home.
These are all types of pet.

budgie

cat

dog

goldfish

guinea pig

hamster

rabbit

tortoise

pick

If you **pick** someone or something, you make
up your mind which one you want.
The king picked his bravest knight to fight the dragon.

Choose means the same as pick.
*Anita wanted to choose a library book
about dolphins and whales.*

If you **pick** flowers, fruit, or vegetables, you take them
from where they are growing.
The princess picked some flowers.

If you **gather** them, you collect them together from different places.
Let's gather all the apples that have fallen from the trees.

picture

There are different kinds of picture.

A **drawing** is something you draw with a pencil or crayon.

A **painting** is a picture that someone has painted.

A **photo** is a picture taken with a camera.

A **cartoon** is a drawing that tells a joke.

A **map** is a drawing of part of the world.

A **portrait** is a picture of a person.

A **poster** is a large picture or notice for everyone to read.

piece

A **piece** of something is part of it.
Would you like a piece of cake?

A **bit** is a small piece of something.
The plate smashed to bits on the floor.

Here are some words you can use to talk about pieces of things.

a **slice** of bread

a **lump** of sugar

a **dollop** of jam

a **scrap** of cloth

a **crumb** of bread or cake

a **grain** of sand

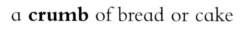

pull

If you **pull** something, you get hold of it and make it come towards you.

As Jake pulled the rope, the basket went up in the air.

If you **drag** something, you pull it along the ground.

Jack walked along, dragging the giant's sword behind him.

If you **tug** something, you pull it hard.

Stop tugging my arm!

If you **tow** a car or boat, you pull it behind you.

They towed our car to the garage.

If you **stretch** something, you pull it to make it longer, wider, or tighter.

The washing line was stretched tight.

If you **draw** curtains, you pull them to open them or close them.

a b c d e f g h i j k l m n o **p** q r s t u v w x y z

79

push

When you **push** something, you use your hands to move it away from you.
Johnny pushed the cat off the bed.

When you **press** something, you push hard on it.
Rebecca pressed the red button to see what would happen.

If you **shove** something, you push it hard.
The crowd pushed and shoved.

If you **poke** something or someone, you push them hard with a stick or your finger.
The baby just poked me in the eye!

If you **nudge** someone, you push them with your elbow.
I nudged Billy and pointed to the frog under the table.

If you **stick** something sharp into a thing, you push the point in.
What happens if you stick a pin in a balloon?

put

If you **put** something in a place, you move it there.
Where did you put the scissors?

You can use these different words to talk about putting things somewhere.

If you **leave** something somewhere, you let it stay where it is.
You can leave your bag here.

If you **place** something somewhere, you put it there carefully.
Samir placed his hand on my shoulder.

If you **lay** something somewhere, you put it down carefully.
Now lay the cloth on the table.

If you **arrange** things, you put them in order or make them look tidy.
Alex arranged the books on the shelf.

If you **pile** things, you put a number of them on top of one another.
The baby piled up the bricks into a tower.

If you **hang** something, you fix the top of it to a hook or nail.
Hang your coat on one of the hooks.

quiet

If someone or something is **quiet**, they make very little noise, or no noise at all.
Sam spoke in a quiet voice.

If someone or something is **silent**, they do not talk or make a sound at all.
Everyone was silent when the queen walked in.

Soft means gentle and quiet.
We could hear soft music.

Here are some other words for quiet sounds.

To **hum** means to make a low sound like a bee.

To **murmur** means to speak softly.

To **patter** means to make light tapping sounds.

To **purr** means to make a gentle murmuring sound like a cat when it is pleased.

To **rustle** means to make a gentle sound like dry leaves being blown by the wind.

To **tick** means to make the sound of a watch or clock.

To **whisper** means to speak very softly.

The opposite of **quiet** is **loud**.

run

When you **run**, you use your legs to move quickly.
Here are some other words that mean run.

To **dash** means to run because you are in a hurry.
We dashed across the road in the rain.

Rush means the same as dash.
Emily rushed downstairs to answer the phone.

If people **race**, they have a contest to find out who is the fastest.

To **scamper** means to run quickly.
Rabbits scamper to their burrows.

To **scurry** means to run with short steps.
The mice scurried across the floor.

When a horse **gallops**, it runs as fast as it can.
When a horse **trots**, it runs quite slowly.

a b c d e f g h i j k l m n o p q **r** s t u v w x y z

sad

If you are **sad**, you are not happy.
Unhappy means the same as sad.

You can also use these other words.

glum

Why are you looking so glum?

heartbroken

He was heartbroken when he thought his cat was lost.

upset

There's no need to get upset.

If you are **disappointed**, you feel sad because
something you were hoping for did not happen.
I am disappointed that we lost the game.

The opposite of **sad** is **happy**.

safe

If someone is **safe**, they are free from danger.
The chicks felt safe in the tree.

To **protect** someone or something means to keep them safe.
The bird protected the chicks from the cat.

Something that is **safe** is not dangerous.
Is that ladder safe?

Harmless means the same as safe.
William's dog barks a lot but it is harmless.

Tame animals are not wild or dangerous.
These mice are very tame.

To **save** means to free someone or something from danger.
Please save the cat from falling!

Rescue means the same as save.
The firefighter rescued the cat from the tree.

a b c d e f g h i j k l m n o p q r s t u v w x y z

say

When you **say** something, you use your voice to make words.
What did you say?

When you **speak**, you say something.
Could you speak more slowly?

When you **talk**, you speak to other people.
Rebecca talked to her friend Anita.

Here are some other words to do with saying things.

When you **ask** something, you put a question to someone
or say that you want something.

When you **answer**, you speak when someone calls
you or asks you a question.
'What's your name?' the cat asked. 'Alice,' she answered.

When you **reply**, you give an answer.
'Can we go to the park?' Jack asked. 'In a little while,' his mother replied.

When you **tell** a person something,
you pass on a story, news, or instructions.
Peter is good at telling jokes.

When you **promise**, you say you will really
do or not do something.
He promised to send a postcard from India.

When you **whisper**, you speak very softly.

When you **mumble**, you speak so that you are not easy to hear.

When you **shout**, you speak very loudly.

When you **complain**, you say that you are not pleased about something.

see

When you **see**, you use your eyes to get to know something.
How many balloons can you see?

If you **notice** something, you see it and think about it.
Did you notice the balloon in the shape of a strawberry?

If you **spot** something, you notice it.
Can you spot the differences between these two pictures?

If you **glimpse** something, you see it for only a very short time.
I glimpsed a castle through the trees.

If you **watch** something, you look to see what happens.
We watched a man juggling balls.

shake

When a thing **shakes**, it moves quickly up and down
or from side to side.
Jumbo was so scared of the mouse he was shaking all over.

If you **shiver** or **shudder**, you shake because you are
cold or frightened.

If a person or animal **trembles**, they shake gently, especially
because they are frightened.

Quiver and **quake** mean the same as tremble.

If something **wobbles**, it moves in an unsteady way from side to side.
The table started to wobble.

shout

If you **shout**, you speak very loudly.
'Get off the grass!' he shouted.

If you **call** someone, you speak loudly
so that they will come to you.
Didn't you hear me call you?

If you **cry** or **yell**, you shout loudly.
A man was stuck in the tree, yelling for help.
'Help, help!' he cried.

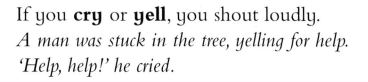

If you **scream**, you cry out loudly,
often because you are hurt or afraid.
We all screamed on the ghost train!

If you **cheer**, you shout to show how much you
like someone or because you are very pleased.
When our team scored, we all cheered.

show

If someone **shows** you how to do something, they do it so that you can watch them.
Alex showed me how to make a cake.

When someone **teaches** you to do something, they show you how to do it.
My dad is teaching me to ride a bike.

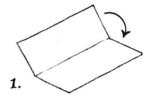

When someone **explains** something, they make it clear so that people will understand it.
I'll explain the rules of the game.

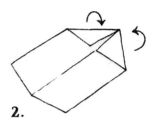

When someone **tells** you how to do something, they give you the information you need to do it.
These instructions tell you how to make a paper aeroplane.

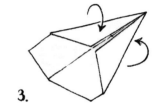

When you **show** something, you let it be seen.
Show me your new bike.

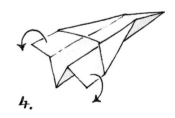

If you **display** something, you show it.
The latest videos are displayed in the shop window.

When you **point**, you show where something is by holding out your finger towards it.
Point to the lolly you want.

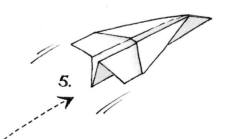

shut

To **shut** means to move a cover, lid or door to block an opening. *Have you shut the door?*

To **close** means the same as to shut.

If you **slam** a door, you shut it loudly.

If you **lock** a door or lid, you fasten it so it cannot be opened without a key.

The opposite of **shut** is **open**.

sleep

When you **sleep**, you close your eyes and your body rests as you do every night.
When you are **asleep**, you are sleeping.

These words are all to do with sleeping.

If you are **sleepy** or **tired**, you want to go to sleep.

To **drop off** or **nod off** means to go to sleep.

To **doze** means to sleep lightly.

To **take a nap** means to have a short sleep.

When you **dream**, you see and hear things in your sleep.

If someone **snores**, they breathe very noisily while they are sleeping.

When you have finished sleeping, you **wake up**.

slide

To **slide** means to move smoothly over
something slippery or polished.
People were sliding on the ice.

You can **skate** on ice too.
We went skating at the ice rink.

If a car **skids**, it slides without meaning to.

If you **slip**, you slide suddenly
without meaning to.
The clown slipped on a banana skin.

If something **slithers**, it slides
as it moves along.
A snake slithered along the ground.

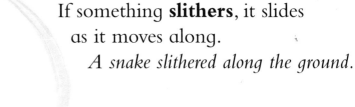

94

small

Small things are not as big as others of the same kind.
I just want a small piece of cake.

Little means the same as small.
In the basket was a little puppy.

Short means not long.
Emma has short hair.
It can also mean not tall.
Robbie is the shortest boy in the class.

Tiny means very small.
There are tiny ladybirds on my book.

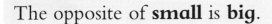

The opposite of **small** is **big**.

a
b
c
d
e
f
g
h
i
j
k
l
m
n
o
p
q
r
s
t
u
v
w
x
y
z

smell

When you **smell** something, you use your nose to find out about it.
Can you smell the roses?

If you **sniff** something, you smell it.
The dog sniffed happily at the leaves.

When something **smells**, you can find out about it with your nose.
Your socks smell awful.

Perfume is a liquid with a nice sweet smell.
A **scent** is a perfume.
A **scent** is also an animal's smell, that other animals can follow.

A **stink** or **pong** is a nasty smell.
You can say that something with a nasty smell is **smelly**.

soft

Things that are **soft** are not hard or firm.
The princess loved her soft bed.

Something that is **fluffy** has soft hair, fur, or feathers.
A fluffy yellow chick hopped out.

Something that is **squashy** is easy to press out of shape.
The banana has gone squashy.

Something that is **floppy** is soft and not stiff.
Katie was wearing a big floppy hat.

The opposite of **soft** is **hard**.

sound

A **sound** is anything that can be heard.
A **noise** is a loud sound.

bang   bleep   bubble   buzz   clang   click   crackle   crunch   drip

fizz plop rattle ring rumble splash tick toot whirr whistle

a
b
c
d
e
f
g
h
i
j
k
l
m
n
o
p
q
r
s
t
u
v
w
x
y
z

99

space

Space is everything beyond the earth,
where the stars and planets are.
Here are some words you can use if you are talking or
writing about space.

A **spacecraft** or **spaceship** is a machine that can carry
people and things through space.

An **astronaut** is a person who travels in a spacecraft.
An astronaut wears a **spacesuit**.

A **space station** is a kind of spacecraft that stays in space. People
live on it for a time to do experiments to find out about space.

The **stars** are the tiny, bright lights you see in the sky at night.

The **sun** gives the earth heat and light. It is a star,
and the earth moves round it.

A **planet** is any of the worlds in space that move around a star.

The **moon** moves around the earth once every twenty-eight days.
You can often see the moon in the sky at night.

Asteroids are very small planets that
move around the sun.

start

When you **start**, you take the first steps in doing something.
The frogs started jumping on the lily pads.

When you **begin**, you start something.
The first frog began to cross the pond.

If you **set out** or **set off**, you start a journey.
Marmaduke's family waved goodbye as he set off on his voyage.

The opposite of **start** is **stop** or **end** or **finish**.

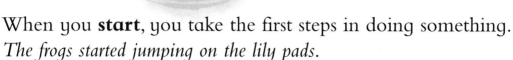
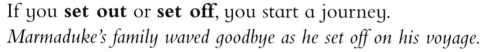

a b c d e f g h i j k l m n o p q r s t u v w x y z

stop

If a person or thing **stops** doing something,
they do not do it any more.
Will these frogs ever stop jumping?

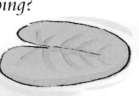

If something that is moving **stops**,
it comes to rest.
*The boat stopped when it bumped
into the lily pad.*

When you **finish**, you come to the end of something.
Once you finish this page, turn over.

To **halt** means to stop.
The frog halted when he saw the fish.

The opposite of **stop** is **start**.

strange

If something is **strange**, it is not like anything you have seen or heard before.
A strange creature came out of the spaceship.

If something is **unusual** or **odd**, it seems strange.
What an odd name!

Something **funny** seems strange.
There's a funny smell in the kitchen.

These words also mean strange.

curious

peculiar

extraordinary

strong

Strong people or animals are healthy and can carry heavy things and work hard.
Are you strong enough to lift a bull?

Mighty and **powerful** mean very strong.
He gave a mighty blow with his hammer.

Something **strong** is hard to break or damage.
We tied the boat with a strong rope.

If something is strong and will last a long time, you can say that it is **tough** or **sturdy**.
Mandy has a new pair of tough boots.

The opposite of **strong** is **weak**.

sure

If you are **sure** about something, you know it is true or right.
'I'm sure I locked the lion's cage,' thought the zookeeper.

Certain means the same as sure.
Are you certain you know the right answer?

Positive means the same as sure.
I am positive that my money was in my coat pocket.

If you are sure something happened or will happen, you can say that
it **definitely** or **certainly** happened or will happen.
Yes, I definitely locked the door.

surprise

A **surprise** is something that you did not expect.
What a lovely surprise!

If something **surprises** you, it is something that you did not expect.

If something **shocks** you, it gives you a sudden nasty surprise.

If something **amazes** or **astonishes** or **astounds** you,
it surprises you very much.
Samir was astonished to see a lion jumping over the wall.

talk

When you **talk**, you speak to other people.
Don't interrupt while I'm talking.

If you **chat** with someone, you have a friendly talk with them.
I chatted with our neighbour.

If you **chatter**, you talk too quickly or too much.
Daniel is always chattering in class.

When people **discuss** things, they talk about them.
We've been discussing the best way to make a spaceship.

When people **argue**, they talk about things they do not agree on.

If people **gossip**, they talk a lot about other people.

taste

The **taste** of something is what it is like when you eat or drink it.
I don't like the taste of cheese.

A **flavou**r is a type of taste.
What flavour of crisps do you want?

If something tastes nice, you can say that it is **delicious** or **tasty**.
This ice cream is delicious.

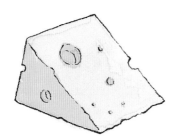

Here are some different kinds of taste.

Sugar and honey have a **sweet** taste.

Lemons have a **sour** taste.

Curry has a **hot** and **spicy** taste.

tell

If someone **tells** you something, they pass on news or instructions or a story.
The storyteller began to tell his tale.

When someone **explains** something, they make it clear so that people will understand it.
Joanna explained the rules of the game to Alex.

When you **promise**, you say you will really do or not do something.
You promised we could go swimming.

If you **warn** someone, you tell them that there is danger.
Dad warned us not to go too near the river.

If you **announce** something, you tell everyone about it.
At assembly, Mrs Doyle announced that she would leave at the end of term.

If someone **tells** you to do something, they say you must do it.

If someone **orders** you to do something, they tell you to do it.
The king ordered his men to enter the forest.

thin

Something that is **thin** does
not measure much from
one side to the other.
The trees were tall and thin.

Narrow means the same as thin.
A narrow path leads through the forest.

A **thin** person or animal does
not weigh very much.
Although the knights were thin,
they were strong and brave too.

Slim and **slender** both
mean thin and graceful.
You can also say that
a thin person is **lean**.

The opposite of **thin** is
thick or **fat**.

think

When you **think**, you use your mind.
Can you think of the answer?

If you **think** something, you have
an idea or opinion.
I think we should go now.

Here are some other words to do with thinking.

If you **concentrate**, you think hard
about something.
Be quiet, I'm trying to concentrate.

If you **believe** something, you feel sure
it is true or real.
Do you believe in ghosts?

If you **expect** something, you think it is
very likely to happen.
I expect there will be lots of people in the park.

If you **imagine** something, you make a
picture of it in your mind.
Imagine you are standing on a giant's hand.

If you **remember** something, you bring
it back into your mind when you want to.
I can't remember her name.

throw

When you **throw** something, you make it leave your hand and move through the air.
I'll throw the ball and you try to catch it.

If you **toss** something, you throw it somewhere.
We tossed some bread to the ducks.

If you **fling** something, you throw it without being careful about it.
She ran into her room, flinging her coat onto the bed.

To **bowl** means to throw a ball towards the person batting in cricket.
It's my turn to bowl.

a
b
c
d
e
f
g
h
i
j
k
l
m
n
o
p
q
r
s
t
u
v
w
x
y
z

touch

If you **touch** something, you put your fingers on it.
The plates are hot, so don't touch them.
If you **feel** something, you touch it to find out what it is like.
I can feel a bump on my head.

These are words for different ways of touching a person or thing.

If you **cuddle** someone you love, you put your arms
closely round them.

If you **kiss** someone, you touch them with your lips.

If you **pat** something, you tap it gently with your hand.

If you can **reach** something, you can stretch out to touch it.

If you **rub** something, you press your hand on it
and move it backwards and forwards.

If you **scratch**, you rub your fingernails over
your skin because it itches.

If you **stroke** something, you move your hand gently along it.

If you **tickle** someone, you keep touching their
skin lightly so that you make them laugh.

Here are some words you can use to say what
something is like when you touch it.

soft   hard   prickly   furry   smooth   rough

wet   dry   lumpy   slimy   hot   cold

tree

These are all different kinds of tree.

holly

oak

fir

larch

horse chestnut

willow

sycamore

palm

pine

turn

When something **turns**, it moves round.
All the different wheels began to turn.

To **spin** means to turn round and round quickly.
Let's spin a coin to see who starts.

To **twirl** means to turn round and round quickly.
She twirled round as she danced.

When you **twist** or **screw** something, you turn it
round so that you can take it off or put it on.
You need to twist the lid off.

vegetable

These are all different kinds of vegetable.

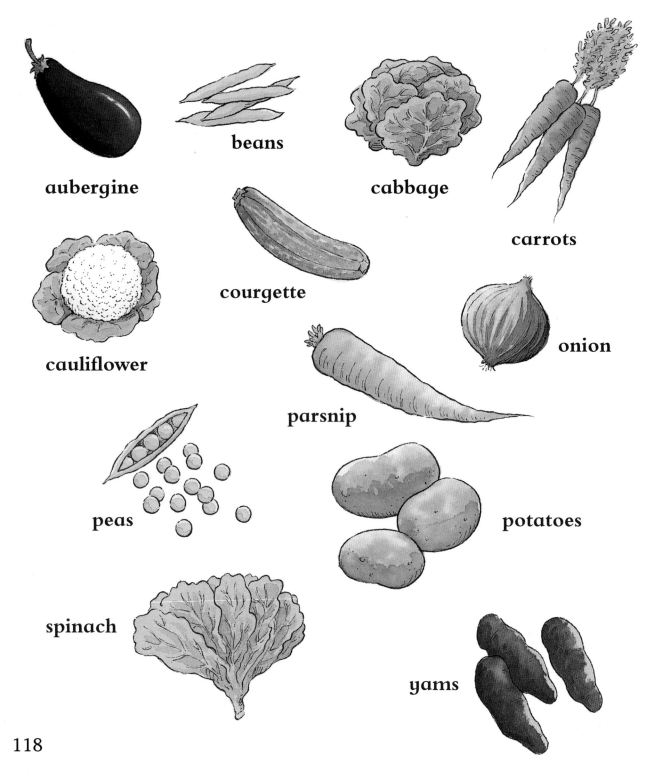

beans

aubergine

cabbage

carrots

courgette

cauliflower

onion

parsnip

peas

potatoes

spinach

yams

walk

When you **walk,** you move along by putting one foot in front of the other.

You can use these words to talk about different ways of walking.

If you **stride**, you walk with long steps.

If you **march**, you walk like a soldier, with regular steps.

If you **tiptoe**, you walk on your toes very quietly or carefully.

If you **creep** somewhere, you walk very slowly and quietly so no one will hear you.

If you **limp**, you walk with difficulty because there is something wrong with your leg or foot.

If you **stagger**, you walk in an unsteady way as if you are just about to fall.

water

Big areas of water

A **sea** is a very large area of water.

An **ocean** is a very big sea.

A **lake** is a large area of fresh water with land all around it.

A **reservoir** is a type of lake that has been specially made to store drinking water.

Small areas of water

A **pond** is a small lake.

A **pool** is a small area of water.

A **puddle** is a small pool of rain water.

Water that flows

A **river** is a lot of water that moves naturally and flows to the sea across the land.

A **stream** is a small river.

A **brook** is a small stream.

A **canal** is a type of river that has been specially made for boats to travel along.

a b c d e f g h i j k l m n o p q r s t u v **w** x y z

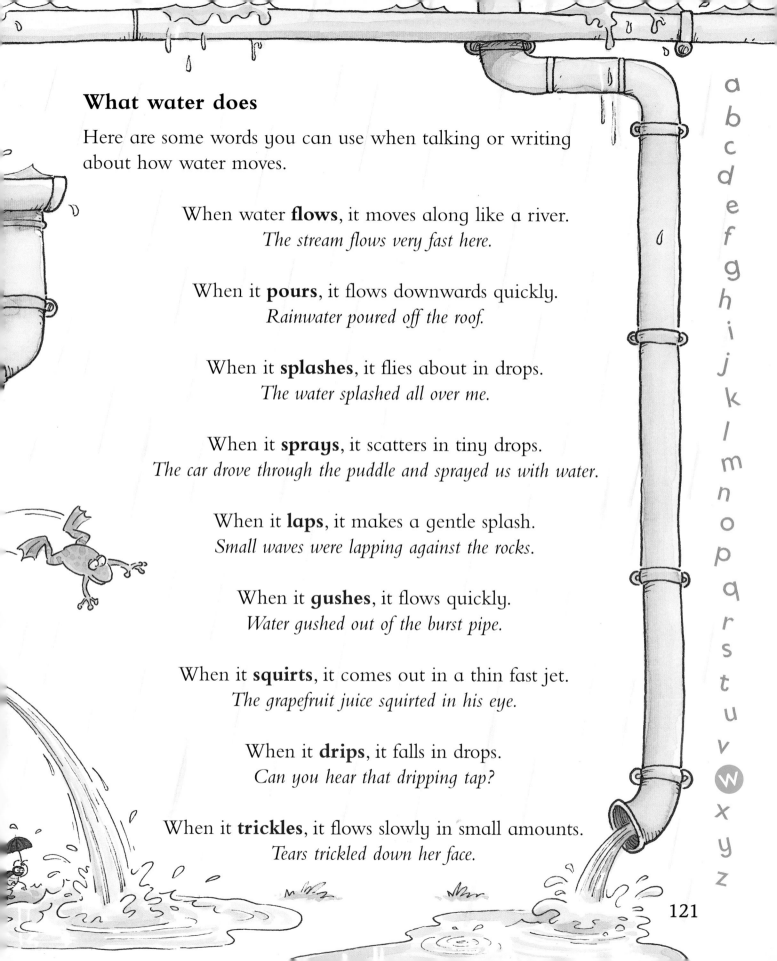

What water does

Here are some words you can use when talking or writing about how water moves.

When water **flows**, it moves along like a river.
The stream flows very fast here.

When it **pours**, it flows downwards quickly.
Rainwater poured off the roof.

When it **splashes**, it flies about in drops.
The water splashed all over me.

When it **sprays**, it scatters in tiny drops.
The car drove through the puddle and sprayed us with water.

When it **laps**, it makes a gentle splash.
Small waves were lapping against the rocks.

When it **gushes**, it flows quickly.
Water gushed out of the burst pipe.

When it **squirts**, it comes out in a thin fast jet.
The grapefruit juice squirted in his eye.

When it **drips**, it falls in drops.
Can you hear that dripping tap?

When it **trickles**, it flows slowly in small amounts.
Tears trickled down her face.

a b c d e f g h i j k l m n o p q r s t u v w x y z

weather

These are all different kinds of weather.

wet

If something is **wet**, it is covered in water, or it has water in it. These words mean very wet.

soaked *We all got soaked in the rain.*

soggy *The ground is very soggy.*

These words mean slightly wet.

damp *The towel is still damp.*

moist *Keep the soil moist to help the seeds grow.*

The opposite of **wet** is **dry**.

young

A person or animal that is **young** was born not long ago.

These are words for young people.

A **baby** is a very young child.

A **child** is a young boy or girl.

A **boy** is a male child or young adult.

A **girl** is a female child or young adult.

These are words for young animals.

A **calf** is a young cow.

A **chick** is a baby bird.

A **cub** is a young lion, tiger, fox, or bear.

A **duckling** is a young duck.

A **foal** is a young horse.

A **kid** is a young goat.

A **kitten** is a young cat.

A **lamb** is a young sheep.

A **piglet** is a young pig.

A **puppy** is a young dog.

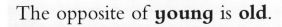

The opposite of **young** is **old**.

Index

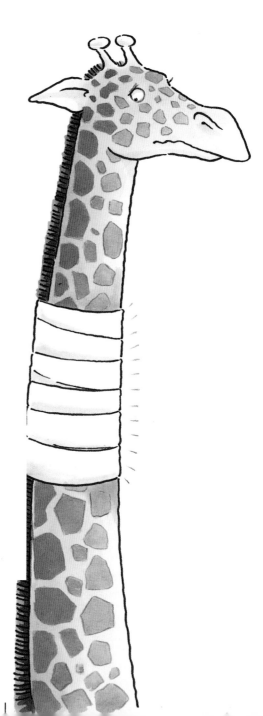

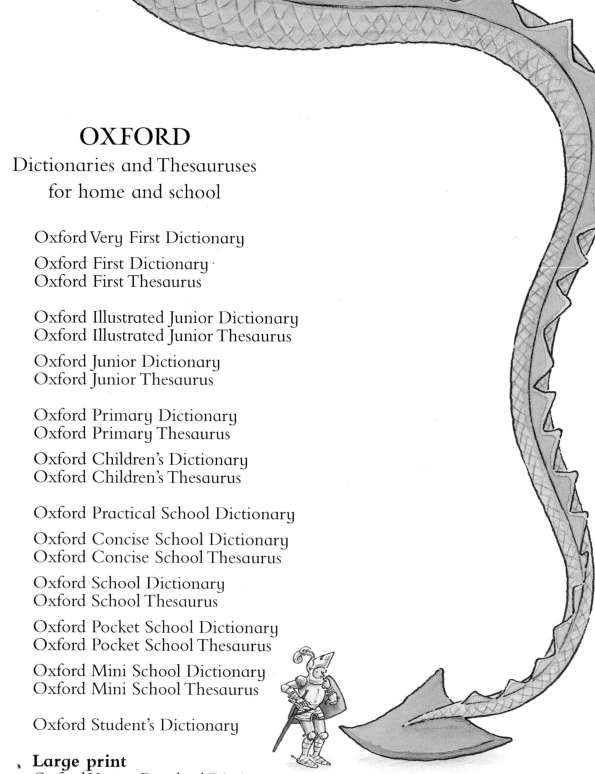

OXFORD

Dictionaries and Thesauruses
for home and school

Oxford Very First Dictionary

Oxford First Dictionary
Oxford First Thesaurus

Oxford Illustrated Junior Dictionary
Oxford Illustrated Junior Thesaurus

Oxford Junior Dictionary
Oxford Junior Thesaurus

Oxford Primary Dictionary
Oxford Primary Thesaurus

Oxford Children's Dictionary
Oxford Children's Thesaurus

Oxford Practical School Dictionary

Oxford Concise School Dictionary
Oxford Concise School Thesaurus

Oxford School Dictionary
Oxford School Thesaurus

Oxford Pocket School Dictionary
Oxford Pocket School Thesaurus

Oxford Mini School Dictionary
Oxford Mini School Thesaurus

Oxford Student's Dictionary

Large print
Oxford Young Readers' Dictionary
Oxford Young Readers' Thesaurus